I0467892

The 4 Essential Habits

For a Sustainably Viable Business

Christopher Gleadle

Index

What is Sustainability?

So much is spoken about, and so much is written about Sustainability, yet to most, it is largely misunderstood. A common mistake is to see it as just being green and to know just what your carbon footprint might be: remembering to recycle, save electricity and gas. While these are constituents, they, on their own are not Sustainability.

Sustainability is to understand the interdependence of your environmental footprint, your social footprint, and how, the combined impact of the two create largely hidden waste and so cost on your balance sheet, and risk to economic shock as well as your long-term viability – commonly spoken about as the triple bottom line of: Environmental, Social and Financial. With visibility given to the interdependent connections between your environmental footprint and your social footprint, in a material, financial and opportunistic way, you create stability and growth for your business, the company you work for, and therefore mitigate the vulnerability to your own personal family security.

Why Sustainability Matters

In a world where the extended supply chains of companies, small as well as large, are extended across the globe the provenance of products and services is often questionable: a claim on efficacy is often given lip service.

Your journey to understanding how easy and resource efficient robust Sustainability actually is will deliver you outstanding competitive advantage. With carbon footprints measured correctly, analyzed with meaning, across your products, your services, buildings, transport – indeed your value chain, you will be more efficient, and effective. This will translate to creating more value for your customers as you learn to see them through the eyes of their customers because you will simply and easily see the connections. Customers will become allies in the creation of new revenue streams, and you will learn that sharing value becomes a powerful tool to enter new markets. Indeed, you will see and understand new ways of marketing and selling products and services, where it is the service that holds greatest value, while you retain ownership of the product.

By learning to see your business in three dimensions, you will see waste that hereto was hidden from view. You will discover opportunities for innovation, for example, not just in the durability and recyclability of the product, but in its design for transport and use to reduce interconnected resource burn extending your value to your market further to enhance profits.

The social dimension of sustainability is also important to any organisation and there are many challenges in measuring the social sustainability of production systems, particularly around the treatment of labour and the impact on communities. It may also be important to address consumer health and safety considerations for particular products. Ambitious organisations may attempt to address the social and psychological impacts of products on consumers. Additionally, understanding the social impact through your supply chain, will allow you to discover innovation opportunities, efficiency opportunities, effectiveness opportunities and give your products and services integrity. Your reputation surely being the most valuable asset you have.

Why Sustainability matters – in short because understood correctly, implemented robustly, Sustainability is a business model that enhances your ability to capture, create and deliver more value. It reduces the barriers to growth that are so common in business. It creates an environment for growth and allows you to make better, more informed decisions on spend. It helps you serve your customers better and helps you make better, more enduring profits. It creates Sustainable Viability.

Your Journey

The 4 Essential Habits for a Sustainably Viable Business

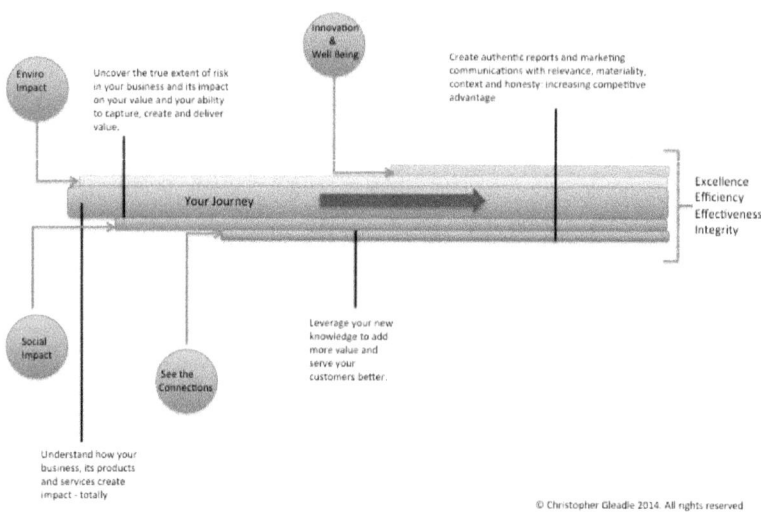

Sustainability and the creation of Sustainable Viability **(S.V.)** are not about bolting on something else to your business. It is not changing your strategy for meeting your goals, desires wants and needs. Far from it. What it is is an enhancement to what you do already. It is creating a system of actions, habits, measured and made accountable to expose waste, expose risk and spotlight opportunity.   With experience it is as natural and as vital as keeping a close check on the cash flow, for Sustainable Viability is about freeing up your cash flow for investing in more efficient, more effective ways to run your business.

So often, Sustainability, and being green is seen only as cutting costs: well cutting costs is vital. To do more with less, and I can show you how. But, I have never seen a company yet become great because it can cut costs better than anyone else. Sustainable Viability is about growth too. It is about innovation, creativity and serving your customers better. Being able to communicate in a material, relevant and authentic manner, with honesty and provenance clearly demonstrated. And, when the deliberate **SV** processes are implemented on a day-to-day basis, both through natural processes of the business, engagement of staff, customers, suppliers etc., it gathers information that will only enhance the value of the business.

It is creating a system of actions, habits, measured and made accountable to expose waste, expose risk and spotlight opportunity. With experience it is as natural and as vital as keeping a close check on the cash flow

Ultimately, it must always be about your story, and your uniqueness – your journey. The value **SV** is going to add is being able to make your journey sustainable and allow you to beat the market in a highly charged competitive market place. And, even if you are a start up, or very small SME, do not allow being a small business spoil the view of what **SV** can add to you and your competitive advantage. Quite the opposite, be excited that it is easier to understand and implement than you ever thought and will give you the competitive advantage to extend your journey of growth and Sustainable Viability.

Habit – 1 Environment: understand how your products and services create impact

Best strategies for a business are to make clear choices and the allocation of its resources, this being comprised of: ' the steady accumulation of frameworks promising to unlock the secret of competition advantage' – Walter Kiechel: The Lords of Strategy, Boston MA – Harvard Business School.

To begin you need to see all your processes, products and services from a waste perspective and start to understand the interdependence of the functions and business units: to see where functions unintentionally conspire to destroy value.

For example, working with an SME, it took just a short while to identify over £100K of wasted expenditure in a meeting with two separate functional managers. By seeing the business in a holistic manner, and understanding how the two functions were budgeted, it was quick to visualize how each function was organized according to what worked best for each manager. The unintentional consequence was huge waste – exceptional unnecessary cost.

So, carbon foot printing brings the whole personnel structure together, from the boardroom to the copy room. And, while for the process to be adopted and work successfully it has to be embraced by the CEO and the board, the real drivers for efficiency and the exclusion of waste is from the main body of the business: its people, who on a day to day basis are the experts in their own job and make the products, deliver the service, engage with the customers.

Where to start

It follows we need to understand where the company is, and create a base line measurement in order to start understanding what can be achieved. With the creation of a baseline measurement it is clear we need to understand where the business intersects with the environment, with emissions and therefore energy use and to evaluate what matters most and so prioritize objectives and goals. This process needs to be conducted from the top down and the bottom up: it needs to be tactical as well as strategic.

Additionally, a quality engagement process begins inside the company where each person is accountable for a new metric defined around efficiency and the reduction of waste and so creating fresh opportunities for innovation towards a leaner operation, products and services.

What gets measured gets managed. Conversely, what gets measured badly gets managed badly. This is a particularly sore point, for; it is very common to see loosely written commitments from companies with throwaway metrics. The point and the opportunity are missed. As for the outside world, 'lip-service' reporting, commonly known as green washing, no matter how well meaning, shows the world there is no understanding in the business to what is really happening. Indeed, a common mistake is to not know how or what Key Performance Indicators should be set, since prescriptions are copied from others. It is about your journey, not any one else's. It is common, even in FTSE 100 companies for Key Performance Indicators to be misunderstood, for data to differ between a Sustainability report and a report to the Carbon Disclosure Project. For example, one large company lost 103,000 tCO2e* in one report. Do not be fooled that because a company is throwing vast resources at Sustainability, they are entirely in control of what they do.

---

*To give a consistent measure of global warming, greenhouse gases are always expressed in terms of CO2. Emissions are grouped as CO2 equivalent and expressed in tonnes (tCO2e). For a list of greenhouse gases and their respective global warming potential (GWP) see Sustainable Growth Through Sustainable Business, Christopher Gleadle 2011.

Key Performance Indicators are important for they assist in delivering meaning to what you are measuring. You understand what it is you want to know. For example, the total electricity usage in a business for a year, and expressed as emissions on its own is meaningless. Emissions expressed on a graph with the cost of making those emissions starts to give meaning. The emissions with costs compared to productivity schedules starts to show the energy needed per unit of production, and so on. You now start to see the impact of production, and hence, the impact on your customer. Thus, using the methodology of Life Cycle Analysis you make the connections between impact emissions and how to reduce the per unit of production cost and you start to see how you can create more value, and deliver more value to your customer.

So, it is not just carbon foot printing, because, for a board to make judgment calls, it needs information. The more frequent the information the better the insight to trends and patterns. Therefore, the higher the frequency of information the better the judgment calls.

Moreover, one of the main stumbling blocks to attaining real efficiency gains are the barriers that are constructed inside companies - the silos, which are naturally created by individuals and groups of individuals, as illustrated earlier with the SME. To work effectively, these barriers for growth need to be broken down, and the silos removed. As we have already said, the company needs to be looked at in three dimensions and everyone needs to understand the interdependence of things that makes the company work, which delivers the products and services in a timely and efficient manner. For, if these barriers are not removed, efficiency change in one department may cause higher waste in another if not properly monitored and verified: efficiency must be effective too!

Therefore, what we now begin to see is that 'eco-efficiency' need not be delivering a return on investment as fast as it could if the processes and initiatives are random and disjointed – not effective. For example, buildings and facilities management is no exception to this rule and includes consideration and interdependencies of not just the buildings themselves, but the services, inventory and people who service and use the buildings. By understanding the entire eco-system of building use, connected to a product or service flow highlights waste and impact and shows the road to innovation to capture, create and deliver more value.

For example, consider the interdependence of:

- Energy and water use
- Internal Environment (building appeal, health & wellbeing)
- Pollution
- Transport
- Materials
- Waste
- Management Processes
- Inventory
- Supply chain
- Embodied Emissions, waste and impact

An example: while understanding LED lamps burn less energy, and financial capital is spent changing over to their use, consider too how the lighting is switched and how the office space is orientated to maximise use of natural light. See the connections from a holistic point of view in order to maximize investment through robust measurement and analysis.

"If the mass flowing out is less than the mass flowing in then there has to be a stream unaccounted for, which is typically a waste process. It is through carrying out these exercises that the savings you can make become most apparent."

Lastly, for this section, I wish to illustrate how making connections will highlight how to make efficiency, effective. I will attempt to use a Personal Computer (P.C): something all businesses of all sizes use. When purchasing a P.C, there are many considerations to take into account. Its functionality, what it is to be used for, how long the technology will be relevant for the use, but also consider what other effects the purchase may have as to choice. How much electricity does it use? How much electricity does the software need to use for processing? How long will the machine be idle? What are its normal hours of production?

From a use point of view, any worthwhile manufacturer should be able to supply facts and figures as to energy consumption for maximum usage to idle usage. This will guide you towards more informed decision making by taking into account the whole life cost of ownership against price and meeting the need of function: efficiency, and effectiveness. Understanding the resource usage will nudge you toward better habits to maximise efficiency, so making the efficient choice, effective. For surely, the IT you purchase has an impact on your customer too. We will continue this example in the following sections, building the whole picture for you to understand how to see the connections.

Habit 2 – Uncover the true extent of risk

In reducing risk and elevating revenue it is vital you understand the interdependence between the bottom line impacts of Environmental and Social and the conspiring risk that hereto has a hidden affect on your balance sheet – the financial bottom line. Additionally, how understanding the nexus between the environmental and social impacts creates a world of opportunity for you, and everyone dependent on your business for financial security.

As we have already started discussing, the area that is likely to be the highest area of cost and risk to your business is your supply chain. This too has the greatest bearing on your ability to be creative, innovative and have direct affect on your provenance.

Therefore, it is vital to understand where your risk may lay, for until now, it has sat unseen, yet could have explosive power to shatter your business. There are many examples where risk, previously unseen has caused explosive power to destroy value.

Example: a well-known, sports apparel manufacturer. When child labour was found in the supply chain, their value was destroyed over night. However, with action taken, investment made into local communities, schools and healthcare centers, their reputation became restored. (Are your brand, and your financial strength so strong you could withstand such an economic shock?) However, more importantly, what also was highlighted was the amount of waste in the supply chain. For, what was discovered was material to make shoes was supplied at a rate to make three shoes, for every pair that was actually made. Once highlighted, $750M a year in wasted expenditure was stemmed.

In the clothing sector, for example, we often still see reports where there is a race to the bottom in employment practices with absence of minimum wage or a living wage, dangerous working conditions, and long hours worked for such minimum reward.

There are clearly established International Labour Organisation protocols in addition to the UN Human Rights charters with clear and transparent methods for auditing to maintain high-risk suppliers. There are many examples of poor supply chain management, yet when addressed led to huge improvements in management of key risks and the removal of vast waste streams.

"human rights due diligence"- has already become a permanent entry in the lexicon of international business. Professor John Ruggie Representative of the UN Secretary-General for Business and Human Rights, Professor of Harvard Kennedy School

Supplies from areas of conflict and high-risk, have impact on the communities, environment and employees of those areas and creates your exposure to the risk of complicity in human rights abuses or military coups if you purchase, even indirectly, from such areas of high risk. And, while conflict affected purchasing typically only affects mineral extraction and exploration for example - and how that can affect local environments, bio-diversity, water, land grabs and resource exploitation without consent, to name but a few - it is incumbent upon businesses, through governance, and director responsibilities to understand the nature of risk. For, is it not correct, that directors, under the Companies Act 2006 (amended) have a duty to report anything material that could damage the future value of the business.

'to provide insight into the entity's main objectives and strategies, and the principal risks it faces and how they might affect future prospects.' 2013 Companies Act amendment

In assessing risk, business is increasingly required to know and understand fully the nature of its exposure via comprehensive due diligence. But, do not be alarmed. This is simpler than it sounds. For a typical SME, to start, construct a simple questionnaire to your supply chain asking relevant questions and highlighting the nature of risk and of opportunity, to create a more cohesive and collaborative framework to capture, create and deliver more value.

However, for due diligence, at its core, it is to know, and understand the risks stemming from likely community action, or likely risks of climate related disturbances to supply and cost volatility. To ignore these issues would be to fatally weaken your reputation, your license to operate and build the potential for economic shock if contingency plans are not in place. How can you have contingency plans to abate risk if you do not know what the risks are in the first place? Additionally, to demonstrate your understanding demonstrates authenticity and provenance. It heightens trust and demonstrates value.

How can you have contingency plans to abate risk if you do not know what the risks are in the first place?

Supply chain management is progressively more about partnership and cooperation and less about imposing standards and codes of practice. This is true whether for a manufacturer and / or services provider, across all sectors.

Furthermore, it is important also to briefly look at legislative risk, that you directly cause, or may trickle down the supply chain. Yet through more partnership and cooperation relationship risks can be abated. For example, more and more governments pursue 'green' strategies, and see a tax shift as an instrument to achieve their goals. It is therefore worthwhile to understand what the tax regimes are in the markets with which you exist and want to sell. Social taxes may exist, which are reduced in return for new sources of public revenue from the introduction of taxes such as:

- Carbon Taxes
- Green Duties
- On imported goods
- Severance taxes on extracted resources
- Product taxes
- Waste disposal taxes
- Landfill taxes and site value taxes

Following on, we must take a moment to see your risks in terms of risk to your customers. Increasingly relevant in the SME space is the Carbon Disclosure Supply Chain Reports.

"Suppliers that do not measure, quantify, and manage their greenhouse-gas emissions will soon see their business move to competitors that can provide better information and clearer evidence of change."
Carbon Disclosure Project (CDP Supply Chain Report 2012)

Where to start

Establish measurable targets and goals, and obtain the information back from your target source. Set the answers against your targets and goals, and work with suppliers to improve and support your performance. And, do not forget to report performance in a simple, relevant and contextual manner. Back up statements with the evidence you have gathered: no different to financial statements. Prove it, and make it material.

The purchase of a P.C., continued.

Where can the risk be in that? Once again, the risk is probably hidden from you. For example, common constituents of electronic equipment are what are abbreviated in the Sustainability world, and that of Conflict Minerals, as 3TG. Simply, this is Tin, Tantalum, Tungsten and Gold. Find out if the supplier has a source trace for the minerals that make up their P.Cs. If not, do they have plans to obtain a source trace. For, such minerals, if sourced via countries such as the Democratic Republic of Congo, the money paid could well have gone to support armed conflict, the destruction of environments, bio-diversity and the communities reliant on those natural resources.

Additionally, through understanding the source of elements for the manufacture of a PC, you start to understand the embedded emissions in the products you buy. Embedded emissions are the emissions, costs and waste put into the production and supply of the purchase before you take account of the use phase. This is important to understand, as here is an impact on your business, which you could be passing on to your customers. Yet, if connected properly, could be an area of efficiency gain, effectively. Furthermore, when building customers and suppliers into collaborative allies, here too is an area of opportunity where you can build in recycling or rehabilitation revenue to set off against the purchase price so improving the whole life cost. An opportunity to once again free cash flow and innovate.

So, keep it simple: look at decisions as three-dimensional connections where you can improve efficiency and effectiveness to improve costs, cash flow and revenue.

Habit 3 – Leverage your newfound knowledge.

"Often value is increased by combining a product with services, or by the complete substitution of the product with a service" Alex Osterwalder

On the exciting journey, that is your journey, you will now be learning how to do more with less, and understand the hidden risks material to your business. What you have to do now is learn how to harness that knowledge and deliver it in a material, contextual and relevant manner. Expose and create the opportunities by removing the barriers for growth. As we have already discussed too, Sustainable Viability is more than the ability to make cost cuts. It is about knowing your risks, freeing cash flow and driving innovation to capture, create and deliver more value for greater profits.

By understanding your carbon emissions, your waste, water and other resource use, you can turn your attention to streamline your processes, your production, and your transport and support services that supply and support your customers.   This includes streamlining your supply structure, from understanding the impact your suppliers have both on your business and therefore your customers.

Additionally, you have started to understand the questions you need to ask of yourselves and the answers will help you serve your customers better. For, you will now be looking at what your customers are achieving on their journey, and importantly on their journey for Sustainable Viability. This will fall in to two areas. Customers that are taking note on Sustainability, and customers that are not.

For those who are on a sustainability journey, understand where they are, where they were and why they are doing it. For a smaller business, you may find ways of assisting them to improve. And, by communicating with your customer in a new and fresh way, what you are inadvertently doing is building closer ties to the customer. You are finding out more about them than you probably knew before. It is giving you another reason to call, to make contact. Importantly, you start to understand who their customers are, and how they see **SV** helping their customers. From these discussions can efficiency and effectiveness be combined to see your customer through the eyes of their customer. You will gain a deeper understanding as to the need and the value you make to them. But also, you will uncover needs previously not understood. You can deliver greater service to your customer for creating value, and so enhanced profits.

An example of an SME who took this approach: The equipment they (and others) supplied to customers was replaced with updated, more technologically advanced equipment about every few years. Working with them, we designed a new service where they did not just install, but became de installers too – taking away all the waste, which included a great deal of 3TG (as discussed earlier) for recycling and re-use. It was agreed to share the value of the new income stream with their customers, which in itself increased the value of the supplier relationship by reducing the whole life cost of supply and maintenance. They reaped a positional and value advantaged position from the competition.

A natural extension to this, and is quite an old business model really, is maintaining ownership of the product. For example, in the supply of a product, it is likely the customer wants the use of the product, or in other words, just wants to extract the value that product will deliver to their business. Therefore, is it not reasonable that instead of selling manufactured goods, lease them out on a service contract? The customer pays for the service, the use. At the end of the products useful life, there is now the opportunity to replace the old product with the new and updated, while removing the old and putting it into a secondary cycle of use - use from either supply to another customer where the product is appropriate, or to rehabilitate the equipment, or completely recycle into the input of another production stream.

The result of such action is to naturally improve the durability and recyclability of the product – thus enhance the quality and value proposition. The connections to this habit have far reaching outcomes to abating resource use and extraction, reduced need for oil and gas, lower environmental impact through landfill, pollution, water use and associated taxes. This is not an exhaustive list but illustrates the connections to lowered impact and elevated value, returned in the form of increased profits, better environmental conditions and better social conditions.

Making connections

Furthermore, by making the connections, not only can you capture new value, but create and deliver new value too. And, for many processes across business this thinking is relevant internally. Look at the manufacturing processes and the waste stream across the processes. Take the waste and recycle immediately back in as an input. This has the effect of reducing, through swapping out for virgin material, cost. It also further reduces the risks of input price volatility and input risk from input disruption from climate or social related risks.

Yet, it does not just have to be a manufacturing process. Having looked at the fuel costs for the car fleet for an SME there were many ways of reducing the costs – indeed a twenty five percent reduction was achieved. But, by taking a holistic view, and understanding the connections, we discovered a training need for the Sales Team in appointment making. Seeing the connections resulting from the initial task of fuel management, the sales and management training gave greater efficient and effective return on investment, freed up cash flow and elevated the productivity of the sales team, which increased sales.

Furthermore, leveraging your newfound knowledge also enables you to see how new markets can be entered without taking you away from your purpose. What I mean here is what we call industrial symbiosis. Simply put, one businesses' waste is another businesses' input. Cheaper inputs and reduced waste management costs conspire in turn to strengthen competitiveness. Additionally, it creates demand for technologies that enables the exchange of materials and energy and knowledge. Notwithstanding the additional branding and reputational advantages delivering competitive advantage.

Additionally, through leveraging your newfound knowledge you increase your pressure on cost avoidance through avoided land fill for example with associated taxes. This therefore begins to complete your circles of reduced impacts, environmentally, socially and financially because of more Sustainably Viable behavior.

An SME: over a three year period waste to landfill fell to just over eleven percent. Yet this is only part of the story as overall waste was reduced by over forty percent. This delivered significant income through recycling and reuse as well as reductions in expenditure through landfill taxes etc. Importantly, reduced too were the emissions associated with waste movement and waste to landfill.

And, since we are now illustrating the connections, and behaviors that flow amongst a Sustainable Lifecycle Analysis **(SLCA)** we seek increases in revenue opportunity with no investment risk and known operational costs because of the transparency created in Habits 1 & 2.

The purchase of a P.C. continued.

What we also need to consider is what can the functionality enable? Do we choose just for the specific need, or can it be used for a wider purpose if we take more functionality, even though it costs more initially?

Here we need to look at what the P.C. can potentially enable you to do. For example, it can enable you to take up the use of teleconferencing. This reduces dramatically your environmental impact, and cost of travel. It could allow also for some home working with teleconferencing, reducing commuting time and cost, as well as environmental and social impact that is the result. Additionally, could a strategy of more people telecommuting negate the need for such expansive offices? Can we divest ourselves of office space? Is it better to rent space out to other small businesses' and bring in another income stream?

- Avoid some staff commuting & increase productivity
- Avoid costly work related travel & increase productivity & well-being
- Reduce Heating Ventilation and Air Conditioning Impact
- Reduce lighting impact in buildings
- Reduce space requirement – remove / redeploy / let / sublet for income

The above list is not exhaustive, yet we clearly see less need for buildings and less transport but develop greater access to productivity gains.

Habit 4 - Create authentic reports and communications for outstanding competitive advantage

The process of reporting compels businesses to look at their value chains and disclose material information and risks. Herein lies the greatest advantage to investors: while standard financial reports are often no more than a superficial, 2-dimensional snapshot of a company's present and future, sustainability reporting goes much further, providing businesses and investors with a comprehensive 3-dimensional picture of how sustainable a company's business model really is.
Ernst Ligteringen - Chief Executive of Global Reporting Initiative.

Sustainable Viability for your business and your life security is reliant on all the parts working together smoothly, completely in an orchestrated manner. Sustainability, time and again helps oil the machine, and leveraged properly delivers Economic Profit. As McKinsey, a consultancy company, have reported in a recent paper, Economic Profit is a Strategic Yardstick you can't afford to ignore.

What is Economic Profit?

Economic profit is what is left over after subtracting the cost of capital from net operating profit – so includes the impact of the visible and hidden costs. The higher the Economic Profit the more Sustainably Viable your business is, and so suggests taking account of the triple bottom line – Economic, Environmental and Social.

Reporting and Communicating

First understand, before making yourself understood. Stephen R Covey, The Seven Habits of Highly Effective People

Reporting is the culmination of your continual improvement, reporting with meaning and context to all those who have a material interest in your business. It too is the reference manual for future proofing your business against risk, and cost. Additionally it is the manual with which all staff can refer, reading it in context and relevance to their work. It is the reference manual with which investors can see the true nature and strength of your business, with proven lowered risk it leads to easier access for capital, and lower costs. And, it is the reference manual for your customers to understand your excellence, efficiency, effectiveness and your integrity – your provenance (a highly valuable asset).

Some still say that until Sustainability translates into shareholder value it will never gain traction. Well, it does. For example: investors want long-term risk adjusted returns, and increasing evidence suggests Environmental Social Governance (ESG) - the term applied to Sustainability in the finance arena - factors manifest themselves as investment risk and opportunities to impart value creation in portfolio companies. ESG is therefore increasingly material to the investment process. The global worth of professionally managed assets that incorporate ESG factors had reached $13.6 trillion and rising (Global Sustainable Investment Alliance (GSIA), as at the end of 2011).

Reporting is the reference manual for your customers or your investors or indeed anyone with a material interest in your business to understand your excellence, efficiency, effectiveness and your integrity – your provenance (a highly valuable asset).

The relevance to an SME is the journey, your journey. For example, in a recent PwC survey for the Principles of Responsible Investment entitled Integration of ESG & Governance issues in M&A (Mergers & Acquisitions) Transactions, Trade Buyers Survey Results, shows that poor performance on ESG factors are used as a lever to reduce the value of a business by as much as ten percent. It being assumed, excellent ESG governance is accounted for in the selling price. Furthermore, once the demand for ten percent discount is exceeded, the willingness to do the deal may well be removed altogether. This suggests that the sale agreement for a £40M company could be affected by £4M for poor ESG performance – if the deal goes ahead at all. (£4M is a great deal of money for having not taken sustainability seriously). And, 80% of deals have shown a reduced valuation, or the deal has not gone ahead based on poor ESG factors.

Ultimately, Sustainability performance is becoming inextricably linked to financial value, whether a public or private business, of all sizes. And, in the pursuit of a more sustainable and just world, it is the translation of that vision, delivered in appropriate language to the appropriate stakeholders where currently misunderstanding happens.

"poor performance on ESG factors are used as a lever to reduce the value of a business by as much as ten percent."

Serving Customers better through Innovation and Well-Being

Additionally, excellent, authentic reporting heightens the inclusive nature of a business. As we have discussed previously, we break down the barriers, the silos that restrict growth. And, through research, time and again, Sustainability has shown to achieve more cohesive and more productive teams reducing the cost base, driving innovation and serving customers better.

Moreover, multiple academic and business research consistently indicates, heightened employee engagement has shown to improve the well-being of employees (reduction in sick days, absenteeism and improve morale), as well as improve motivation, creativity, innovation and loyalty to the brand – making that brand one that employees are more likely to recommend to others as an organisation to work for. Thus, lower employee churn to aid retention of top-talent so reducing costs, process interruption, improving eco-efficiency and eco-intensity – being effective. Indeed, research further indicates engagement scores directly against earnings per share performance: nearly 28% advantage (Gallup)[1] against competitors: notwithstanding "When employees are positive about their organization's Corporate Social Responsibility commitment, employee engagement rises to 85%." (Sirota)[2]. This set against contra information where fewer than 1 in 3 employees worldwide (31%) are engaged, and nearly 1 in 5 (17%) are actually disengaged (Blessing White)[3].

What this suggests, is the process of Sustainable Viability delivers the capacity to consistently enter into open dialogue and engage employees in sustainability. Furthermore, it galvanizes employees and their actions, to remove the barriers for growth and unleash the potential to make a difference with elevated feelings of self worth. Indeed, this continues to their private lives too; helping them make better choices that serve them, their families, communities and the environment.

Therefore, you now see and understand the importance of authentic reporting. It is essential to break free from the gravity of the mediocre, and rise above the flippant, lip-serving reporting that is the majority to deliver for you outstanding competitive advantage. Your reports will become your user manual for customers, suppliers, and investors – using it as a springboard for growth.

The purchase of a P.C. continued.

We can now identify, measure effectively, quantify and report the benefits it will truly bring to your business, in terms of direct functionality and the positive affects it will enable. The process has given you a great deal more information to make clear, better, more informed judgments on spend and the choice of P.C. to obtain. Apply this thinking to all that you do.

[1]Gallup – State of the American Workplace Report 2008-2012

[2]Sirota Survey Intelligence (2007) – Corporate Social Responsibility Contributes To Bottom Line, Improves Worker Engagement And Customer Loyalty

[3]Blessing White – 2011 Employee Engagement Report

Conclusion – Excellence, Efficiency, Effectiveness and Integrity

McKinsey (a consultancy company) noted: *improving resource productivity is likely to develop structural cost advantage and improve the ability to capture new growth opportunities.*

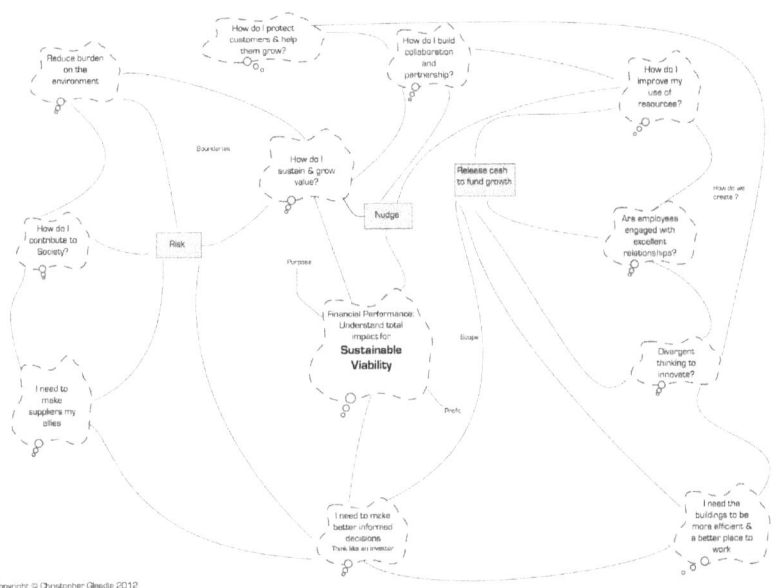

Understanding and seeing the connections for Sustainable Viability

Following the process for Sustainable Viability (**SV**) you are able to see and understand the interdependent connections between your environmental footprint, your social footprint, and how, the combined impact of the two create largely hidden waste, risk and cost on your balance sheet. Furthermore, by connecting inter and intra functions and business units you expose the hidden waste and cost streams and expose fresh opportunities. Additionally you will be able to report in a material, contextual, relevant and honest way. The reports being the user manual to over come your barriers to growth: to capture, create and deliver more value and exploit outstanding competitive advantage.

For the customers you serve, you will be in an easy position to know how to serve them better. You will be able to see their world from their customers' position to create better collaboration – sharing value and creating alliances.

By understanding the interdependencies of The 4 Essential Habits for a Sustainably Viable Business you will beat the market to create security for your business, for your family and all those dependent on your success – wherever they may be. You will make a difference, to make the world a better place to live and create societies with more equality, an environment that is more stable, and bio diversity that is richer. Your business will be run better, capturing more value by using less and be more profitable.

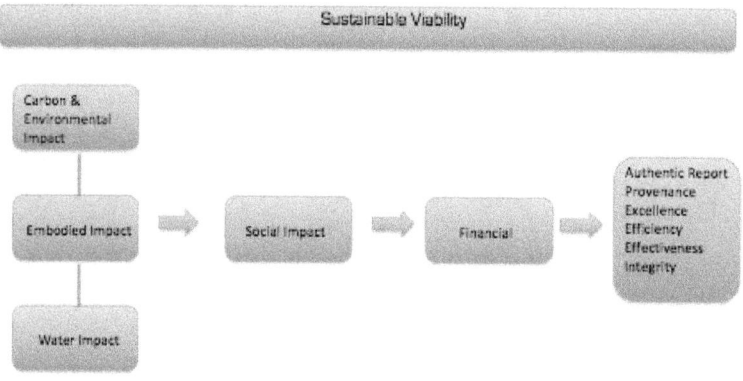

About the Author - Christopher Gleadle

 Christopher's vast commercial background includes working for Fortune 500's as well as creation of his own businesses. Yet, 2007/8 was a key moment in his life with the financial crash. Christopher could see a commercial career can be more fully in tune with that of environmental and bio-diversity protection balanced with greater opportunity for all, if understood and communicated correctly: to mitigate risk, cost and develop fresh growth strategies to further create a more balanced economy and help avoid further financial crashes. His extensive research and experience lead him to write his first 'How To' book: Sustainable Growth Through Sustainable Business. This led Christopher to working on, and contributing to, the leading International Accounting and Reporting Standards (see below for list of public commitments). With the uptake of International speaking, Christopher subsequently became author and co-author to five further books (See below for list). Furthermore, Christopher has papers and articles widely published globally across business, academia and NGO's. Additionally, Christopher has become an experienced international speaker, mentor, trainer and business coach. Ultimately, some people regard Christopher as one of the leading international experts on Sustainability, ESG (Environmental Social and Governance) and Sustainable Viability.

Public Commitments

Greenhouse Gas Protocol Corporate Accounting and Reporting Standard

GHGP Product Life Cycle Accounting and Reporting Standard

GHGP Value Chain (Scope 3) Life Cycle Accounting and Reporting Standard

GHGP Technical Guidance for Calculating Scope 3 Emissions

GHGP Life Cycle Accounting and Reporting Standard ICT Sector Guidance

GHGP Financial Sector Guidance for Corporate Value Chain (Scope 3) Accounting and Reporting

GHGP Agriculture Guidance

Global Reporting Initiative – G4 Standard

BS 8900-1:2013; Managing Sustainable Development of Organisations – Guide

BS 8900-2:2013; Managing Sustainable Development of Organisations Framework for assessment against BS8900-1- Specification

DEFRA Mandatory Reporting Standard

IIRC <IR> Integrated Reporting

GISR (Global Initiative for Sustainability Ratings)– To design and steward a global sustainability (ESG) ratings standard.

Books

Sustainable Growth Through Sustainable Business – Amazon (2010)

Corporate Governance and Sustainability Challenges – IOD (2011)

Social Responsibility – IOD, (2012)

Corporate Governance Perspectives and Sustainability Challenges – IOD (2012)

Business Excellence – Key to Achieving World Class Performance – IOD (2013)

The 4 Essential Habits For a Sustainably Viable Business – CMG (2014)

Christopher Gleadle
Coach, Educator and Advisor in Sustainability

Contact:

+44 (0) 1865 600 154
+44 (0) 7980 087543
christopher@thecmgconsultancy.com
www.thecmgconsultancy.com

www.ingramcontent.com/pod-product-compliance
Lightning Source LLC
Chambersburg PA
CBHW051226170526
45166CB00005B/2062